EARTH SCIENCE—LANDFORMS Need to Know

SilverTip

Rivers and Streams

by Ashley Kuehl

Consultant: Jordan Stoleru,
Science Educator

BEARPORT
PUBLISHING

Minneapolis, Minnesota

Credits
Cover and title page, © mariusz_prusaczyk/iStock; 3, © Ruslan Suseynov/Shutterstock; 5, © r.classen/Shutterstock; 7, © ApostolosGR/iStock; 8–9, © ichael Schmitz/Shutterstock; 10, © damien calmel/Shutterstock; 11, © KaPel92/Shutterstock; 13, © somrak jendee/Shutterstock; 15, © Ravi Natarajan/iStock; 17, © Harvepino/iStock; 19, © Worraket/Shutterstock; 20–21, © Nika Lerman/Shutterstock; 22, © Windzepher/iStock; 23, © JeffGoulden/iStock; 24–25, © charliebishop/iStock; 27, © Robert Bodnar T/Shutterstock; 28, © ArtMari/Shutterstock.

Bearport Publishing Company Product Development Team
President: Jen Jenson; Director of Product Development: Spencer Brinker; Managing Editor: Allison Juda; Associate Editor: Naomi Reich; Associate Editor: Tiana Tran; Art Director: Colin O'Dea; Designer: Kim Jones; Designer: Kayla Eggert; Product Development Assistant: Owen Hamlin

Statement on Usage of Generative Artificial Intelligence
Bearport Publishing remains committed to publishing high-quality nonfiction books. Therefore, we restrict the use of generative AI to ensure accuracy of all text and visual components pertaining to a book's subject. See BearportPublishing.com for details.

Library of Congress Cataloging-in-Publication Data

Names: Kuehl, Ashley, 1977– author.
Title: Rivers and streams / by Ashley Kuehl.
Description: Minneapolis, Minnesota : Bearport Publishing Company, 2025. | Series: Earth science. Landforms: need to know | Includes bibliographical references and index.
Identifiers: LCCN 2024006087 (print) | LCCN 2024006088 (ebook) | ISBN 9798892320535 (library binding) | ISBN 9798892325271 (paperback) | ISBN 9798892321860 (ebook)
Subjects: LCSH: Rivers–Juvenile literature. | Human ecology–Juvenile literature.
Classification: LCC GB1203.8 .K84 2025 (print) | LCC GB1203.8 (ebook) | DDC 551.48/3–dc23/eng/20240307
LC record available at https://lccn.loc.gov/2024006087
LC ebook record available at https://lccn.loc.gov/2024006088

Copyright © 2025 Bearport Publishing Company. All rights reserved. No part of this publication may be reproduced in whole or in part, stored in any retrieval system, or transmitted in any form or by any means, electronic, mechanical, photocopying, recording, or otherwise, without written permission from the publisher. Bearport Publishing is a division of Chrysalis Education Group.

For more information, write to Bearport Publishing, 5357 Penn Avenue South, Minneapolis, MN 55419.

Contents

Gather at the River 4
Flowing Downhill 6
Soggy Sources. 8
Growing and Shrinking 12
Destroying and Building 14
Around and Around 18
Water for Life 22
Amazing Rivers and Streams 26

Rivers and the Water Cycle. 28
SilverTips for Success 29
Glossary 30
Read More 31
Learn More Online 31
Index 32
About the Author 32

Gather at the River

What do Chicago, New York, London, and Shanghai have in common? These large cities were all built along rivers. And they are far from the only ones. For thousands of years, people have made homes near the waterways. Rivers are as much a **resource** as they are a **landform**.

> Every continent on Earth has rivers. Some rivers run steady all the time. Others flow strongly during some seasons. Then, they disappear at different parts of the year.

Flowing Downhill

Rivers are flowing bodies of fresh water. Streams are usually thought of as smaller rivers. Sometimes, a few streams join together to form a river.

These waterways travel downhill, moving thanks to **gravity**. The force pulls the water down and onward.

Larger objects have stronger gravity. Earth's gravity pulls everything on the planet to its surface. In addition to moving water, it keeps people and buildings on Earth.

Soggy Sources

Stream and river water can come from many different sources. Some comes from underground. A spring is a place where water flows up to the surface from below.

Water can also come from a nearby lake. Water may spill out from its banks, sending a river flowing over the ground.

The start of a river or stream is called its headwaters. The other end is the mouth. From there, water pours into a bigger body of water, such as a lake or ocean.

Heavy rains sometimes start rivers. If too much water falls too quickly, the ground can't take it all in. The water begins to form a stream.

The same thing happens when snow melts. The extra water may add to a river. Or it could start a new one.

Glaciers are huge sheets of ice. When they melt, their water can add to rivers or start new ones, too.

Growing and Shrinking

Streams and rivers can change quickly. Extra water can make a river grow. But these waterways can shrink, too. If a place is dry for a long time, a stream or a river can get smaller. It might even disappear.

Average temperatures around the world are rising. The heat is making Earth's water dry up faster. This is causing some rivers to disappear.

Destroying and Building

Rivers and streams can change the landscape around them. As water flows over land, it breaks off bits of dirt and rock. This is called weathering. The water then washes those pieces, called sediment, downstream. This is erosion. Over time, a river can carve new shapes into the land.

The Grand Canyon was once a flat plateau. Over many years, the Colorado River flowed along the same path. It washed away rock, creating the canyon we see today.

The Grand Canyon

A flowing river carries this sediment for a while. Eventually, the river drops the sediment in new places. The rock and dirt can build up around a river's mouth. This creates a **delta**.

Sometimes, rivers flood onto the land around them. This leaves sediment behind even after the water is gone.

> The Nile River empties into the Mediterranean Sea. Near its mouth, the river forms a delta. This is one of the biggest deltas in the world.

Around and Around

The water in rivers and streams is always changing, too. The water cycle is a natural process in which water moves and changes.

Some river water **evaporates** as it flows. The liquid turns into a gas called water vapor. Water moves up into the air in this form.

> Water changes form throughout the water cycle. It becomes liquid, gas, and solid at different points. It is a liquid when it is flowing. Water vapor is a gas. Ice is solid water.

High in the sky, water vapor gathers into clouds. When clouds are full of water, they let go of some. It falls to the ground as rain or snow. Some of this water ends up in rivers and streams. Then, the cycle starts over again.

The same water travels around the world as it moves through the water cycle. It changes again and again. A drop of water in a river today may have been in a cloud when dinosaurs walked the planet.

Water for Life

People need fresh water to live. We use it for drinking and watering crops. People even make electricity from flowing rivers. Since ancient times, people have used rivers to move things and people. We've built cities around rivers to be able to use all that these waterways have to offer.

People build dams to stop moving water. The water is stored for future use. Dams are also used to make electricity from water's movement.

The soil around rivers is good for farming. River sediment holds lots of **nutrients**. Nutrients in the soil near rivers help crops grow.

The Central Valley in California is a big farming area. The Sacramento and San Joaquin rivers provide water for these crops.

About one-third of the vegetables people eat in the United States come from the Central Valley. Two-thirds of the nuts and fruits we eat are grown there, too.

Amazing Rivers and Streams

At their most basic, rivers and streams are simply flowing water. But they do so much as they go. These waterways shape the land and help keep the water cycle going. Rivers and streams support life. We're lucky we have these landforms.

Sometimes, rivers need our help. The Colorado River provides water for 40 million people. But it is drying up because we are taking too much water. People are working on plans to protect the river.

Rivers and the Water Cycle

The water cycle keeps our wet world going. Rivers are a big part of this process.

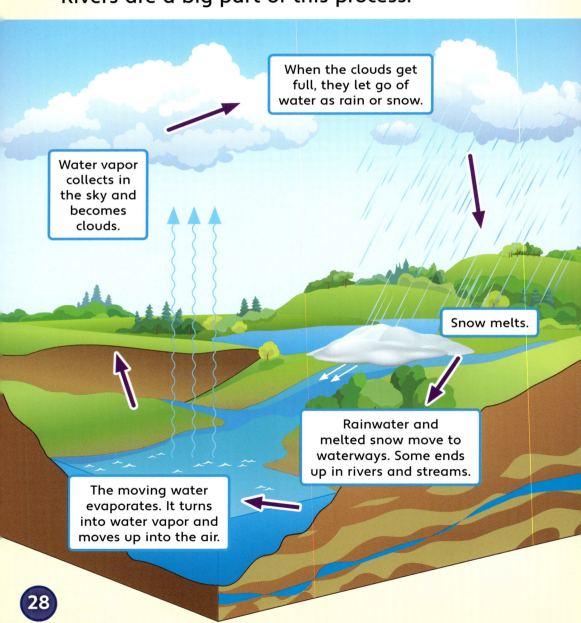

When the clouds get full, they let go of water as rain or snow.

Water vapor collects in the sky and becomes clouds.

Snow melts.

Rainwater and melted snow move to waterways. Some ends up in rivers and streams.

The moving water evaporates. It turns into water vapor and moves up into the air.

SilverTips for SUCCESS

★ SilverTips for REVIEW

Review what you've learned. Use the text to help you.

Define key terms

erosion
evaporate
sediment
sources
water cycle

Check for understanding

Name two sources for rivers and streams.

How can a river change the landscape?

Describe the water cycle. In what ways does Earth's water move?

Think deeper

What role do rivers and streams play in your community? How do you use them?

★ SilverTips on TEST-TAKING

- **Make a study plan.** Ask your teacher what the test is going to cover. Then, set aside time to study a little bit every day.

- **Read all the questions carefully.** Be sure you know what is being asked.

- **Skip any questions** you don't know how to answer right away. Mark them and come back later if you have time.

Glossary

delta a piece of land that forms at the mouth of some rivers before they flow into an ocean or a sea

erosion the carrying away of rock and soil by natural forces, such as water and wind

evaporates changes from a liquid into a gas

gravity the force that pulls all things on Earth toward the ground

landform a natural feature on Earth's surface

nutrients substances needed by plants to grow and stay healthy

resource something, often found in nature, that is useful or valuable

sediment tiny pieces of rock that have broken away from larger rocks

sources the places from which things come

weathering the breaking apart or wearing away of rock and soil by natural forces, such as water and wind

Read More

Agnone, Julie Vosburgh. *Amazing Rivers: 100+ Waterways That Will Boggle Your Mind (Our Amazing World).* Greenbelt, MD: What on Earth Books, 2021.

Finan, Catherine C. *Dams (X-treme Facts: Engineering).* Minneapolis: Bearport Publishing Company, 2023.

Willis, John. *Rivers (Aquatic Ecosystems).* New York: AV2, 2021.

Learn More Online

1. Go to **www.factsurfer.com** or scan the QR code below.
2. Enter "**Rivers and Streams**" into the search box.
3. Click on the cover of this book to see a list of websites.

Index

cities 4, 22
delta 16–17
electricity 22–23
erosion 14
farming 24
gravity 6
headwaters 9
lakes 8–9
mouth 9, 16
ocean 9

rain 10, 20, 28
sediment 14, 16, 24
snow 10, 20, 28
sources 8
springs 8
water cycle 18, 20–21, 26, 28
water vapor 18, 20, 28
weathering 14

About the Author

Ashley Kuehl is an editor and writer specializing in nonfiction for young people. She lives in Minneapolis, MN.